KITTIES TO STITCH & QUILT

15 REDWORK DESIGNS

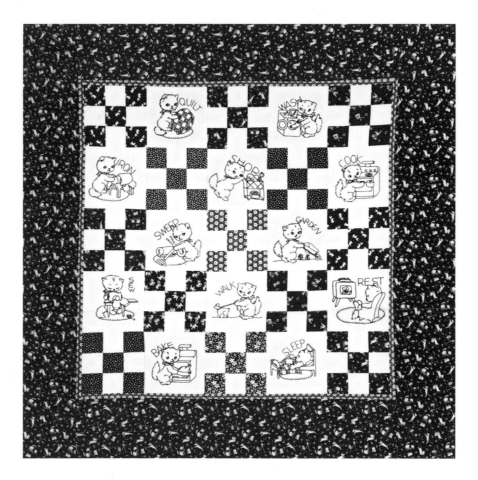

NANCY J. MARTIN

Martingale
& COMPANY

Bothell, Washington

CREDITS

President . . . . Nancy J. Martin
CEO/Publisher . . . . Daniel J. Martin
Associate Publisher . . . . Jane Hamada
Editorial Director . . . . Mary V. Green
Design and Production Manager . . Cheryl Stevenson
Technical Editor . . . . Ursula Reikes
Copy Editor . . . . Karen Koll
Cover Designer . . . . Cheryl Stevenson
Text Designer . . . . Laurel Strand
Illustrators . . . . Laurel Strand, Jil Johänson
Photographer . . . . Brent Kane

That Patchwork Place is an imprint of Martingale &
Company.

DL N5

Kitties to Stitch and Quilt: 15 Redwork Designs
© 2000 by Nancy J. Martin

Martingale & Company
PO Box 118
Bothell, WA 98041-0118 USA
www.patchwork.com

Printed in China
05 04 03 02 01 00   6 5 4 3 2 1

MISSION STATEMENT

We are dedicated to providing quality products and
service by working together to inspire creativity
and to enrich the lives we touch.

DEDICATION

To my grandmother, Margaret Butler Parry, who
taught me to stitch as a young child. I still remember
my first embroidery lesson on Sunday afternoon after
church. I was wearing my only "dress-up outfit" and
had embroidered the stitches through my project onto
my skirt, since I had rested the hoop on my lap. Oh,
how I cried when we had to cut out my first stitches!
Thank goodness she gave me another chance.

ACKNOWLEDGMENTS

To Alvina Nelson of Salina, Kansas, who beauti-
fully quilted the "Kitty Homemaker" quilt.
To Cheryl Stevenson, for her "instant" embroidery.

Library of Congress Cataloging-in-Publication Data
Martin, Nancy J.
    Kitties to stitch and quilt : 15 redwork designs / Nancy J.
Martin.
        p.   cm.
    ISBN 1-56477-309-4
    1. Quilting—Patterns. 2. Patchwork—Patterns.
    3. Embroidery—Patterns. I. Title: Kitties to stitch and quilt.
    II. Title.
    TT835.M27335   2000
746.46'041—dc21
                                              99-058874
                                                  CIP

CONTENTS

INTRODUCTION

Embroidery became popular during the late nineteenth century. Many of the early embroidery designs were from the Royal School of Art Needlework, established in 1872 in Kensington, England. These designs were meant to be elaborately embroidered, although many women preferred to work the designs in a simple outline stitch. The outline stitch was often referred to as the Kensington Stitch.

Much of the simple outline embroidery was suitable for children's quilts. Indeed, many of the designs were from Kate Greenaway nursery books, since at the time designs could not be effectively protected by copyright law. Kate Greenaway was a popular artist of the period. Her little girls in Victorian dresses set a style that is still popular today.

In the early part of the twentieth century, many designs were referred to as "stamped goods" and were available on squares of muslin ranging from 6" to 9". These designs were also called "penny squares" because you could buy them for only a penny. Most emporiums, dry goods stores, and five-and-ten-cent stores had a needlework counter where stamped goods and embroidery floss were sold. I remember when I was a young girl, my grandmother and I made a weekly shopping trip to the five-and-ten-cent store, where she would let me choose a piece of stamped goods to embroider.

Although the designs on stamped goods could be executed in a variety of colors, multicolor embroidery was usually found on pillowcases, dresser scarves, and tablecloths. Most of the small penny-square designs were done in red embroidery and used in children's quilts.

Redwork was first seen in Europe and referred to as "Turkey work." The name was derived from the colorfast dye used to make the floss, probably developed in the area around Turkey. Threads dyed using the Turkey red process were advertised with a logo of a large turkey with the word *red* stamped across its chest.

Penny squares or other stamped goods were sometimes embroidered in other single colors. Sometimes women chose to embroider their work with blue floss, a choice attributed to the early German immigrants. Others speculate that the blue embroidered penny squares were for boys' quilts.

Weekly newspaper columns featuring quilt, needlework, or embroidery patterns began in the late 1920s. Initially they appeared only on Saturday and Sunday, but reader response led some newspapers to publish these columns daily.

Syndicated pattern companies provided content for some of the columns, as discussed in *Twentieth Century Quilts: 1900-1950.* "The most influential of the syndicates, Home Arts and Old Chelsea Station Needlecraft Service, reached millions of women through their pattern lines. Bettina, Hope Winslow, and Colonial quilts were offered by the former, and Laura Wheeler and Alice Brooks were operated by the latter. The reason for such quaint, Betty Crocker-type names was reader appeal. Sending money to a grandmotherly woman seemed so much more personal and more like the old-fashioned, neighborly pattern exchange of an earlier era."[1] The Workbasket was another popular pattern company.

---

1. Thos. K. Woodard and Blanche Greenstein, *Twentieth Century Quilts, 1900–1950* (New York: E. P. Dutton, 1988).

Needlework columns continued to be a popular source of patterns and embroidery transfers into the 1940s for women who lived in rural areas. At a country auction, I was fortunate to win the bid on a box of embroidery and quilt patterns acquired by Mrs. R. W. Showalter of Phoenixville, Pennsylvania. Mrs. Showalter saved all the patterns in their original envelopes, which were postmarked weekly through the 1940s. These patterns were offered in the needlework column of *The Evening Bulletin*, a Philadelphia newspaper. The garment patterns were attributed to Suzanne Lane, while most of the embroidery patterns were from The Workbasket.

Embroidery patterns were offered as transfers that could be heat stamped, using an iron, onto the customer's own fabric. Many different themes were available: state flowers, state birds, plants, nursery rhyme characters, and dogs or cats performing household chores. Many of these transfers were offered in sets of seven: one for each day of the week, presumably to be embroidered on dish towels. The Kitty Homemaker designs most likely originated in the 1940s based on the images of the washing machine, vacuum cleaner, mangle ironer, and shopping cart. Often the days-of-the-week designs related to the nursery rhyme that lists Monday as wash day, Tuesday as ironing day, etc.

Pillowcases were also popular items for embroidery. These designs came in pairs such as His and Hers or Good Morning and Good Night. My favorite set reads "I slept and dreamed that life was beauty/ I woke and found that life was duty."

Embroidery designs, especially redwork, are now enjoying renewed popularity. Many women are relaxing while creating beautiful embroidered linens—a lovely touch of luxury in our busy lives.

EMBROIDERY DESIGNS

KITTY HOMEMAKER DESIGNS

These designs depict Kitty performing a variety of household activities. The designs are sized to fit onto a 6" finished square. They can be used for the quilt projects in this book or other quilt designs and projects that require a 6" finished square.

KITTY DISH TOWEL DESIGNS

During the 1930s and 1940s, many young girls learned to do embroidery on dish towels. Frugal housewives stamped the designs onto bleached flour sacks or feed sacks. A few simple stitches embellished these humble household items.

The three designs depict Kitty drying china, glass, and silver. Because they were designed to be embroidered on dish towels, they are slightly larger than the

Kitty Homemaker designs. If you want to use them in a quilt, look for designs that use a 7½" finished square.

HOT IRON TRANSFERS

The designs for Kitty Homemaker squares and Kitty dish towels are presented on hot iron transfers for stamping on fabric and in black and white drawings for tracing.

To use the hot iron transfers, you'll need a dry iron set for cotton. Carefully center the transfer on the fabric. With firm pressure, hold the iron in place for about ten seconds. Do not move the iron back and forth or you will blur the lines. If the design is large, move the iron and hold again for about ten seconds. Repeat until the whole design is transferred. Place the transfer exactly where you want it on the fabric. Once ironed, the transfer ink is permanent and will not wash out. Transfers can be used several times.

TRACING THE DESIGNS

Once you've used up the hot iron transfers, you can trace the images from the black and white drawings using a lead pencil or transfer pencil. To use a lead pencil, lightly trace the design onto the right side of a piece of fabric. To help you see the design, trace the image onto a piece of paper and tape the paper to a window or use a light table.

To use a transfer pencil, trace the design onto lightweight paper. Place the paper, marked side down, on the fabric and press firmly with a hot iron. Lift a corner of the paper to see if the design has transferred to the fabric. The marks from some transfer pencils will wash out, but others are permanent. Read the manufacturer's directions that came with your pencil.

TIP

Be sure to trace the design so that the words read correctly when stitched. To trace a design with a lead pencil, trace the image as it is shown on the black and white drawing. To trace with a transfer pencil, trace the reverse of the black and white image.

EMBROIDERY

Use good-quality, six-strand embroidery floss and small embroidery needles. The smaller the needle, the finer your stitch will be. You will need a hoop to hold the material taut while you are stitching. Choose a wooden or plastic hoop between 4" and 6" in diameter. If the hoop is too small, you'll have to move it often to complete the design. If the hoop is too large, the square of fabric may not fit well enough to keep it taut.

TIP

If you are right-handed, position the screws or clamps on your left. This will keep the thread from being caught in the screws or clamps. Position the screws or clamps on the right if you are left-handed.

Use two strands of embroidery floss for stitching the designs. To separate two strands from the six-strand embroidery floss, cut the length you want first; about 18" is a good length. Carefully pull out one strand at a time. Put two together to stitch. For Kitty's fur, use

straight stitches on the short lines and small outline stitches on the longer lines. Use additional stitches as indicated below.

Nose	Satin stitch
Pupil	Satin stitch
Rug	Blanket stitch
Flowers	Couched circle
Bubbles	Couched circle

Straight stitch   Outline stitch

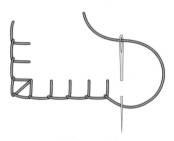

Satin stitch

Blanket stitch

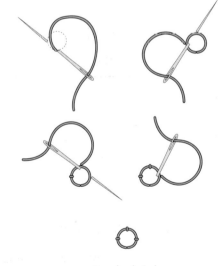

Couched circle

CAUTION

Cover all lines with embroidery stitches because lines may not wash out.

FABRIC SELECTION

FOR EMBROIDERED BLOCKS

Select tightly woven, 100% cotton fabric. Fabric that is loosely woven will not have enough threads to put tiny stitches exactly where you want them. Cut squares 1" larger than necessary and trim them to the correct size after the embroidery is complete.

FOR QUILTS

For best results, select lightweight, closely woven, 100% cotton fabrics. Polyester content may make small patchwork pieces difficult to cut and sew accurately.

Most embroidered quilts were made during the thirties and forties. This was the heyday of rainbow colors and conversation prints or novelty prints. The prints usually had juvenile themes that told a story or depicted a nursery rhyme. We are fortunate now to have access to many reproduction fabrics that mimic the conversation prints. They are available in a variety of colors and are fun to include in a quilt.

Consider the color of floss used for the embroidered blocks when selecting fabric. If blocks are to be done in redwork, then select a variety of red fabrics, as shown in "Nine Patch" on page 17. Red fabrics can also be combined with different colored fabrics, such as green in "Kitty Homemaker" on page 25, or blue and white for a patriotic quilt.

Blue embroidery combines nicely with blue color schemes, as in the blue and yellow quilt "This and That" on page 20. Green embroidery floss, especially the mint green used in the thirties, is another good choice. It blends well with a variety of green fabrics like those shown in "Framed Square" on page 22.

Select the background fabric first. Although the embroidery will be done on a solid white or muslin fabric, you don't need to use the same fabric for the background of the rest of the block or quilt. In "Kitty Homemaker," various light prints serve as the background of the blocks.

I like to purchase an assortment of prints rather than a single red print or a single blue print. Be sure to include both large and small prints, florals, conversation prints, stripes, and polka dots when making your choices. You can also include prints other than the reproduction thirties and forties fabric. Remember that many quilts of that era were made from the scrap bag, so a variety of fabrics from varying periods were used.

The quilt patterns in this book call for fat quarters in assorted colors, in addition to full-length yardage. A fat quarter is an 18" x 21" piece of fabric rather than the standard quarter yard that is cut selvage to selvage and measures 9" x 42". It is a more convenient size to use for cutting squares and strips for the quilts in this book. Look for the basket or bin of fat quarters at your local quilt shop when selecting fabrics.

FOR DISH TOWELS

The cotton fabric used to make quilts is not absorbent enough for dish towels. Towels made from the same plain-woven cotton as flour sacks are wonderful for drying everything from pots and pans to delicate crystal. Look for yardage specifically designed to be used for towels, or purchase ready-made towels. If you are lucky enough to find towel yardage, ¾ of a yard will be ample size for a towel, including turning under the edges.

You can find ready-made towels in houseware and kitchen catalogs or your local needlework, quilting, or department stores. If you can't find "flour sack" towels, look for other plain-weave cotton or linen towels.

PREPARING FABRICS

Make it a habit to wash and prepare fabrics after you purchase them. Then your fabric will be ready to sew when you are.

Wash all fabrics first to preshrink, test for colorfastness, and get rid of excess dye. Continue to wash the fabric until the rinse water is completely clear. Add a square of white fabric to each washing of the fabric. When this white fabric remains its original color, the fabric is colorfast. A cupful of vinegar in the rinse water can also be used to help set difficult dyes. After washing, press the fabric and fold it into fourths lengthwise.

BASIC QUILTMAKING TECHNIQUES

SUPPLIES

ROTARY CUTTER AND MAT: A large rotary cutter enables you to cut strips and pieces quickly without templates. A cutting mat is essential to protect both the blade and the table on which you are cutting. An 18" x 24" mat allows you to cut long strips on the straight or bias grain. You might also consider purchasing a smaller mat to use when working with scraps.

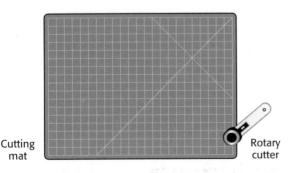

Cutting mat

Rotary cutter

ROTARY-CUTTING RULERS: Use a long, see-through ruler to measure and guide the rotary cutter. One that is 24" long is a good size. Try to find one that includes markings for 45° and 60° angles, guidelines for cutting strips, and standard measurements. Using a specialized ruler improves cutting accuracy, makes quiltmaking more fun, and frees you from the matching and stitching frustrations that can result from inaccurate cuts.

The Bias Square® ruler is critical for cutting accurate bias squares. This acrylic ruler is available as a 4", 6", or 8" square, and is ruled with ⅛" markings. All feature a diagonal line, which, when placed on the bias seam, enables you to cut bias squares.

The Bias Square is also convenient to use when cutting small quilt pieces, such as squares, rectangles, and triangles. The larger 8" size is ideal for quick cutting blocks that require large squares and triangles as well as for making diagonal cuts for half-square and quarter-square triangles.

SEWING MACHINE: Stitching quilts on a sewing machine is easy and enjoyable. Spend some time getting to know your machine and becoming comfortable with its use. Keep your machine dust-free and well oiled.

PINS: You need a good supply of glass- or plastic-headed pins. Long pins are especially helpful when pinning thick layers together.

If you plan to machine quilt, you will need to hold the layers of the quilt together with a large supply of rustproof, size 2 safety pins.

IRON AND IRONING BOARD: Frequent and careful pressing is necessary to ensure a smooth, accurately stitched quilt top. Place your iron and ironing board, along with a plastic spray bottle of water, close to your sewing machine.

NEEDLES: Use sewing-machine needles sized for cotton fabrics (size 70/10 or 80/12). You also need hand-sewing needles (Sharps) and hand-quilting needles (Betweens, size #8, #9, or #10).

SCISSORS: Use good-quality shears, and use them only for cutting fabric. Thread snips or embroidery scissors are handy for clipping threads.

SEAM RIPPER: This little tool will come in handy if you find it necessary to remove a seam before resewing.

ROTARY CUTTING

USE AND CARE OF A ROTARY CUTTER

A rotary cutter has a very sharp blade. It is so sharp that you can cut yourself without even knowing it. If you are not extremely careful, you can also cut other people and objects that you had no intention of slicing. Before you use your rotary cutter for the first time, it is important to know some simple safety rules.

- Close the safety shield when the rotary cutter is not in use.
- Roll the cutter away from yourself. Plan the cutting so your fingers, hands, and arms are never at risk.
- Keep the cutter out of the reach of children.
- Dispose of used blades in a responsible manner. Wrap and tape cardboard around them before placing them in the garbage.

For comfort's sake, think about your posture and the table height as you cut. Stand to cut—you'll find more control than when sitting. Many quilters find they are more comfortable and can work longer if the cutting table is higher than a normal sewing table, so they don't have to bend as they cut. If you work on a table that is placed away from a wall, you can easily walk to another side of the table to make your next cut, rather than moving the fabric or the cutting mat.

If you are left-handed, reverse all cutting directions. Begin by placing the fabric to your left and the ruler to your right. Use a mirror to view the photos. This will help you see the proper cutting alignment.

CUTTING STRAIGHT STRIPS

Rotary cutting squares, rectangles, and other shapes begins with cutting strips of fabric. These strips are then crosscut to the proper dimensions. All strip measurements include 1/4"-wide seam allowances.

To cut strips from the crosswise grain:
1. Fold and press the fabric with selvages matching, aligning the crosswise and lengthwise grains as much as possible. Place the folded fabric on the rotary-cutting mat, with the folded edge closest to your body. Align the Bias Square with the fold of the fabric and place a ruler to the left as shown.

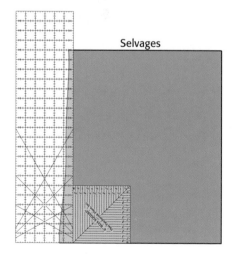

Selvages

2. Remove the Bias Square and make a rotary cut along the right side of the ruler to square up the edge of the fabric. Hold the ruler down with your left hand, placing your little finger off the edge of the ruler to serve as an anchor and prevent slipping. Stand comfortably, with your head and body centered over the cutting. Do not twist your body or arm into an awkward position.

As you cut, carefully reposition your hand on the ruler to make sure the ruler doesn't shift and the markings remain accurately placed. Use firm, even pressure as you cut. Begin rolling the cutter on the mat before you reach the folded fabric edge and continue across. For safety's sake, always roll the cutter away from you. Remember: the blade is very sharp, so be careful!

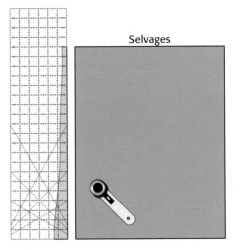

Selvages

3. Fold the fabric again so that you will be cutting 4 layers at a time. Cut strips of fabric, aligning the clean-cut edge of the fabric with the ruler markings at the desired width. Open the fabric strips periodically to make sure you are cutting straight strips. If the strips are not straight, repeat steps 1 and 2 to

square up the edge of the fabric again before cutting additional strips. Don't worry. This adjustment is common.

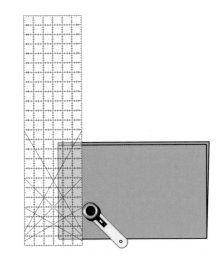

SQUARES AND RECTANGLES

1. Cut fabric into strips the measurement of the finished square plus seam allowances.

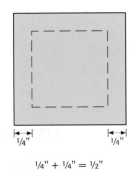

¼" + ¼" = ½"

2. Using the Bias Square, align the top and bottom edges of the strip and cut the fabric into squares the width of the strip.

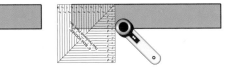

3. Cut rectangles in the same manner. First, use the shorter measurement of the rectangle to cut strips, then use the longer measurement to cut the strips into rectangles.

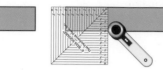

4. To cut a small, odd-sized square or rectangle for which there is no marking on your cutting guide, make an accurate paper template (including ¼"-wide seam allowances). Tape it to the back of the Bias Square, and you will have the correct alignment for cutting strips or squares.

HALF-SQUARE TRIANGLES

Most of the triangles used in the quilts in this book are half-square triangles. These triangles are cut so that the straight grain is on the short edges of the triangle. Cut a square ⅞" larger than the finished size of the short edge of the triangle to allow for seam allowances; then cut the square once diagonally to yield two half-square triangles.

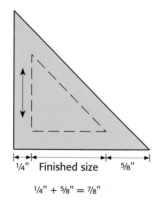

¼" Finished size ⅝"

¼" + ⅝" = ⅞"

1. Add ⅞" to the desired finished size and cut a strip to the measurement.
2. Cut the strip into squares that are the same measurement as the strip width.

3. Cut a stack of squares once diagonally.

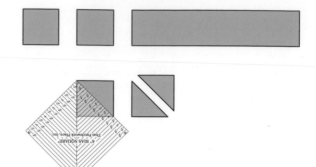

QUARTER-SQUARE TRIANGLES

These triangles are cut so that the straight grain is on the long edges of the triangles. The long sides are placed along the outside edges of blocks and quilts to keep the edges of quilts from stretching. Cut a square 1¼" larger than the finished size of the long edge of the triangle; then cut it twice diagonally to yield four quarter-square triangles.

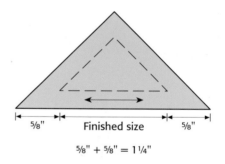

⅝" Finished size ⅝"

⅝" + ⅝" = 1¼"

1. Cut a strip as wide as the desired finished measurement plus 1¼".
2. Cut the strip into squares that are the same measurement as the strip width.
3. Cut a stack of squares twice diagonally.

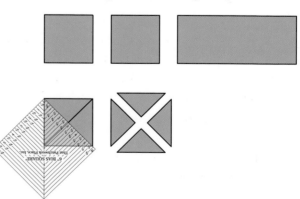

MACHINE PIECING

The most important skill in machine piecing is sewing an accurate ¼"-wide seam. This is necessary for seams to match and for the resulting block or quilt to measure the required size. There are several methods that will help you achieve this.

- Purchase a special foot that is sized so that you can align the edge of your fabric with the edge of the presser foot, resulting in a seam that is ¼" away from the fabric edge. Bernina has a special patchwork foot (#37), and Little Foot makes several special ¼" feet that fit most machines.

- If you have an electronic or computerized sewing machine, adjust the needle position so that the resulting seam is ¼" away from the fabric edge.

- Find the ¼"-wide seam allowance on your machine by placing an accurate template under the presser foot and lowering the needle onto the seam line. Mark the seam allowance by placing a piece of masking tape at the edge of the template and in front of the needle. You can use several layers of masking tape, building a raised edge to guide your fabric. You can also use a piece of moleskin for a raised seam guide.

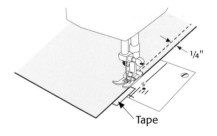

Do the following test to make sure that the method you are using results in an accurate ¼"-wide seam.

1. Cut 3 strips of fabric, each 1½" x 3".
2. Sew the strips together, using the edge of the presser foot or the seam guide you have made. Press seams toward the outer edges. After sewing and pressing, the center strip should measure exactly 1" wide. If it doesn't, adjust the needle or seam guide in the proper direction.

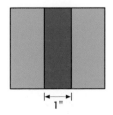

BIAS SQUARES

Many traditional quilt patterns contain squares made from two contrasting half-square triangles. The short sides of the triangles are on the straight grain of the fabric while the long sides are on the bias. These are called bias-square units. Using a bias strip-piecing method, you can easily sew and cut bias squares. This technique is especially useful for small bias squares, where pressing after stitching usually distorts the shape (and sometimes burns fingers). An easy way to cut bias squares is to use squares of fabric. The size of the cut square and the width of the strips are specified in the quilt directions.

NOTE

Quilt directions in this book give the cut size for bias squares; the finished size after stitching will be ½" smaller.

---

1. Layer 2 squares of fabric, right sides facing up, and cut in half diagonally.

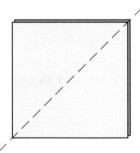

2. Cut into strips, measuring from the previous cut.

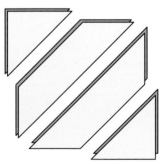

3. Stitch the strips together using ¼"-wide seam allowances. Be sure to align the strips so the lower edge and 1 adjacent edge form straight lines.

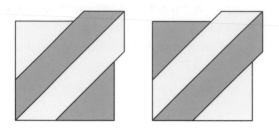

4. Begin cutting at the lower left corner. Align the 45° mark of the Bias Square ruler on the seam line. Each bias square will require 4 cuts. The first and second cuts are along the side and top edges. The cuts remove the bias square from the rest of the fabric. Make these cuts ¼" larger than the correct size, as shown in the series of illustrations below.

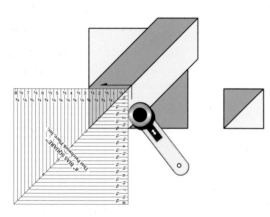

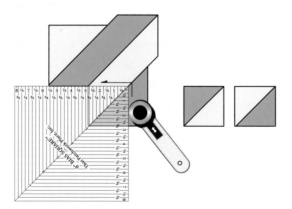

Align 45° mark on seam line and cut first two sides.

5. The third and fourth cuts are made along the remaining 2 sides. These cuts align the diagonal and trim the bias square to the correct size. To make the cuts, turn the segment and place the Bias Square on the opposite 2 sides, aligning the required measurements on both sides of the ruler and the 45° mark on the seam. Cut the remaining 2 sides of the bias squares.

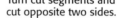
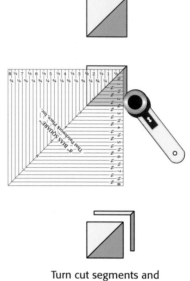

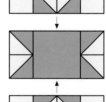

Turn cut segments and cut opposite two sides.

6. Continue cutting bias squares from each unit in this manner, working from left to right and from bottom to top, until you have cut bias squares from all usable fabric.

MATCHING SEAMS

When sewing the fabric pieces that make up a unit or block, follow the piecing diagram provided. Press each group of pieces before joining it to the next unit.

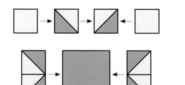

Stitch, then press.   Join units together.

There are several techniques you can use to get your seams to match perfectly.

OPPOSING SEAMS: When stitching one seamed unit to another, press seams that need to match in opposite directions. The two "opposing" seams will hold each other in place and evenly distribute the fabric bulk. Plan pressing to take advantage of opposing seams. You will find this particularly important in strip piecing.

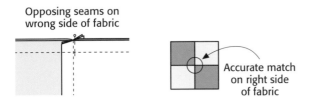

POSITIONING PIN: A pin, carefully pushed straight through two points that need to match and pulled tight, will establish the proper matching point.

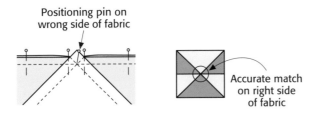

THE X: When triangles are pieced, the stitches will form an X at the next seam line. Stitch through the center of the X to make sure the points on the sewn triangles will not be cut off.

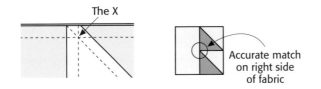

EASING: When two pieces you are sewing together are supposed to match but are slightly different in length, pin the points to match and stitch with the shorter piece on top. The feed dogs will ease the fullness of the bottom piece.

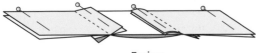

Easing

Inspect each intersection from the right side to see that it is matched. If the seams do not meet accurately, note which direction the fabric needs to be moved. Use a seam ripper to rip out the seam intersection and 1/2" of stitching on either side of the intersection. Shift the fabric to correct the alignment, place positioning pins, then restitch.

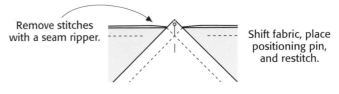

PRESSING

After stitching a seam, press your work. Careful pressing helps make the next steps in the stitching process, such as matching points or aligning seams, easier.

Be sure to press, not iron, your work. Ironing is an aggressive back-and-forth motion that we use on clothing to remove wrinkles. This action can easily pull and distort the bias edges or seams in your piecing. Pressing is the gentle lowering, pressing, and lifting of the iron along the length of the fabric without moving the iron back and forth along the seam. Let the heat, steam, and an occasional spritz of water press the fabric in the desired direction.

CHAIN PIECING

Chain piecing is an assembly-line approach to putting your blocks together. Rather than sewing each block from start to finish, you can sew identical units of each block together at one time, streamlining the process. It's a good idea, however, to first sew one sample block together from start to finish to ensure that you have cut the pieces accurately and that you have the proper positioning and coloration for each piece.

Stack the units you will be sewing in pairs, arranging any opposing seam allowances so that the top seam allowance faces toward the needle and the lower seam allowance faces toward you. Then you won't need to keep checking to see if the lower seam allowance is being pulled to the wrong side by the feed dogs as you feed the fabric through the sewing machine.

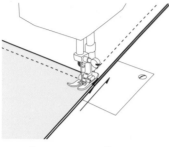

Face top seam allowance
toward the needle
whenever possible.

Feed the units through the machine without stopping to cut the thread. There will be a "stitch" or small length of thread between the units.

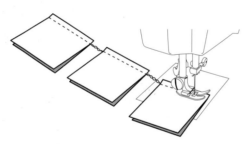

Take the connected units to the ironing board for pressing, then clip them apart. Chain piecing takes a little planning, but it saves you time and thread.

ASSEMBLING BLOCKS

Pin rows of blocks together at strategic intersections to ensure accurate matching when sewing rows together. The process is similar to matching seams within a block. To make the process easier, plan for opposing seams when you press blocks after stitching. Press seams in opposite directions from row to row.

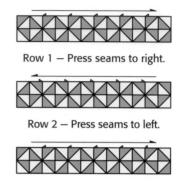

Row 1 — Press seams to right.

Row 2 — Press seams to left.

Row 3 — Press seams to right.

Carefully matched rows of blocks will meet ¼" from the raw edge when rows are sewn together.

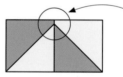

¼" seam allowance
for seam intersection

Use positioning pins to hold seam allowances in place. See page 15. Remove the pin before stitching through the seam intersection.

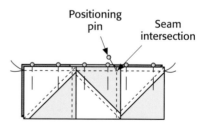

Positioning
pin

Seam
intersection

NINE PATCH

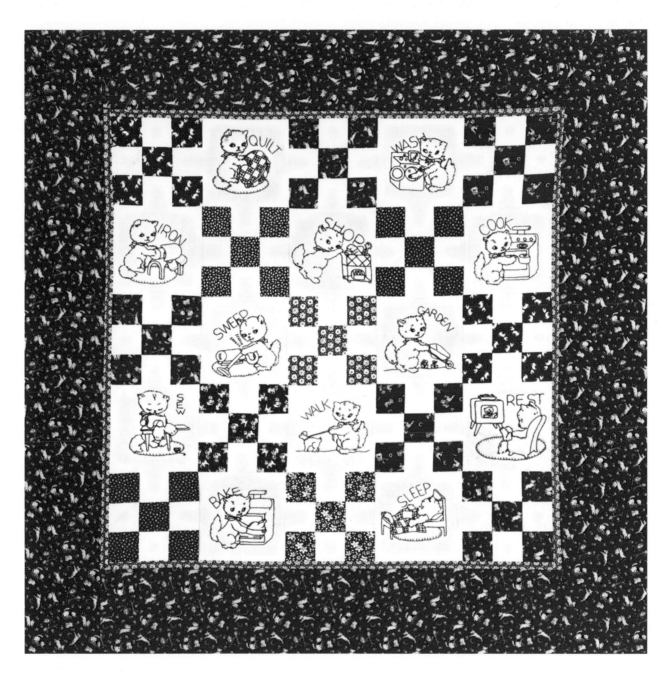

NINE PATCH by Cleo Nollette, 1999, Seattle, Washington, 43" x 43".

6" block   6" block

MATERIALS
42"-wide fabric

1 yd. white solid for embroidery and Nine Patch blocks

1 fat quarter each of 6 different red prints for Nine Patch blocks*

¼ yd. light red print for inner border

1 yd. dark red print for outer border

3 yds. for backing

⅜ yd. of fabric for 182" of bias binding

3 skeins of 6-strand embroidery floss in red

> ** The most economical way to purchase and cut fabric for this quilt is to make two identical blocks from each print and then one extra block from your favorite print. For a scrappier look, like the quilt shown on page 17, add more red prints.*

CUTTING

From the white solid, cut:

    12 squares, each 7½" x 7½", for embroidery blocks

    6 strips, 2½" x 18", for Nine Patch blocks

    12 strips, each 2½" x 9", for Nine Patch blocks

From each fat quarter, cut:

    2 strips (12 total), each 2½" x 18", for Nine Patch blocks

    1 strip (6 total), 2½" x 9", for Nine Patch blocks

From the light red print, cut:

    2 strips, each 1" x 30½", for inner side borders

    2 strips, each 1" x 31½", for inner top and bottom borders

From the dark red print, cut:

    5 strips, each 6¼" x 42", for outer border

DIRECTIONS

1. Transfer the Kitty Homemaker designs to the 12 white squares. Embroider the designs and press the finished blocks. Trim the blocks to 6½" x 6½", centering the design.

2. Join the 2½" x 18" red strips and white strips to make 6 of Strip Set 1. Press the seam allowances toward the red strips. Crosscut each strip set into 4 segments, each 2½" wide. Cut 2 extra segments from the strip set with your favorite red print.

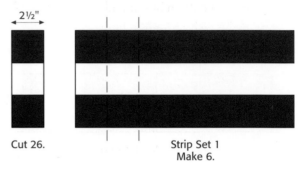

2½"

Cut 26.   Strip Set 1
Make 6.

3. Join 2½" x 9" red strips and white strips to make 6 of Strip Set 2. Press the seam allowances toward the red strip. Crosscut each strip set into 2 segments, each 2½" wide. Cut 1 extra segment from the strip set with your favorite red print.

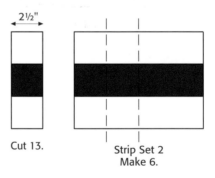

2½"

Cut 13.   Strip Set 2
Make 6.

4. Join matching segments to make a Nine Patch block. Make 2 blocks from each red print, then make an extra from your favorite red print.

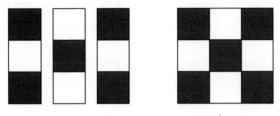

Make 13.

5. Join 3 Nine Patch blocks and 2 embroidered blocks to make each of 3 rows. Press the seam allowances toward the embroidered blocks.

Make 3 rows.

6. Join 2 Nine Patch blocks and 3 embroidered blocks to make each of 2 rows.

Make 2 rows.

7. Join the rows, beginning and ending with a row that has 3 Nine Patch blocks.

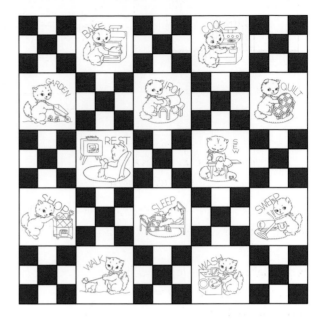

8. Add the 1" x 30½" light red strips to the sides of the quilt top. Add the 1" x 31½" light red strips to the top and bottom of the quilt top.

9. Join the 6¼"-wide dark red strips for the outer border and stitch them to the quilt top following directions on page 29.

10. Layer the quilt top with batting and backing. Quilt as desired.

11. Bind the edges with bias strips of fabric.

THIS AND THAT

THIS AND THAT by Cleo Nollette, 1999, Seattle, Washington, 36½" x 48½".

Block 1
12" block

Block 2
12" block

MATERIALS
42"-wide fabric

¾ yd. white solid for embroidery blocks

1 fat quarter each of 6 blue prints for This and That blocks*

1 fat quarter each of 6 yellow prints for This and That blocks*

1⅝ yds. for backing

⅜ yd. fabric for 178" of bias binding

3 skeins of 6-strand embroidery floss in blue

The quilt on the facing page was made with scraps of additional blue and yellow prints to increase the scrappy look of this quilt.

CUTTING

From the white solid, cut:

   12 squares, each 7½" x 7½", for embroidery blocks

From each blue fat quarter, cut:

   2 squares (12 total), each 5⅛" x 5⅛". Cut once diagonally to yield 24 small triangles.

   2 squares (12 total), each 6⅞" x 6⅞". Cut once diagonally to yield 24 large triangles.

From each yellow fat quarter, cut:

   2 squares (12 total), each 5⅛" x 5⅛". Cut once diagonally to yield 24 small triangles.

   2 squares (12 total), each 6⅞" x 6⅞". Cut once diagonally to yield 24 large triangles.

DIRECTIONS

1. Transfer the Kitty Homemaker designs to the white squares. Embroider the designs and press the finished blocks. Trim the blocks to 6½" x 6½", centering the design.

2. Join 4 small yellow triangles and 4 large blue triangles to make This and That Block 1.

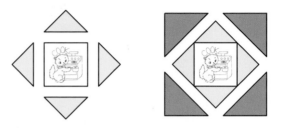

3. Join 4 small blue triangles and 4 large yellow triangles to make This and That Block 2.

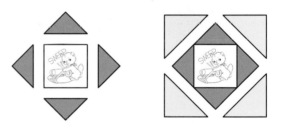

4. Arrange the blocks into 4 rows of 3 blocks each, alternating Blocks 1 and 2. Join blocks into horizontal rows. Join the rows.

5. Layer the quilt top with batting and backing. Quilt as desired.

6. Bind the edges with bias strips of fabric.

FRAMED SQUARE

FRAMED SQUARE by Nancy J. Martin, 1999, Woodinville, Washington, 38½" x 47½".

MATERIALS

44"-wide fabric

1¼ yds. muslin for embroidery blocks and piecing
1 fat quarter each of 10 green prints for piecing*
⅝ yd. green print for borders
1⅝ yds. for backing
⅜ yd. fabric for 184" of bias binding
3 skeins of 6-strand embroidery floss in green

The quilt on the facing page was made with scraps of additional green prints to increase the scrappy look of this quilt.

CUTTING

From the muslin, cut:
  12 squares, each 7½" x 7½", for embroidery blocks
  15 strips, each 1½" x 21", for piecing
  10 strips, each 1½" x 13", for piecing

From the green fat quarters, cut a total of:
  30 strips, each 1½" x 21", for piecing
  5 strips, each 1½" x 13", for piecing

From the green print, cut:
  2 strips, each 4½" x 39", for side borders
  2 strips, each 4½" x 38½", for top and bottom
    borders

DIRECTIONS

1. Transfer the Kitty Homemaker designs to the muslin squares. Embroider the designs and press the finished blocks. Trim the blocks to 6½" x 6½", centering the design.

2. Join the 1½" x 21" muslin strips and green strips to make 15 of Strip Set 1. Press the seam allowances toward the green strips. Crosscut the strip sets into 31 segments, each 6½" wide. Crosscut the remaining strip sets into 20 segments, each 1½" wide.

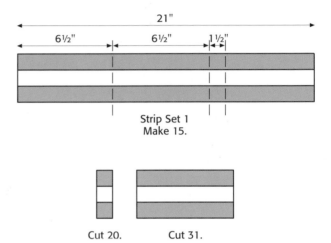

Strip Set 1
Make 15.

Cut 20.   Cut 31.

3. Join the 1½" x 13" muslin strips and green strips to make 5 of Strip Set 2. Press the seam allowances toward the green strips. Crosscut the strip sets into 40 segments, each 1½" wide.

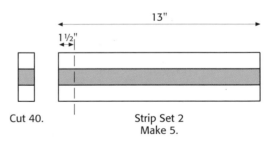

Cut 40.

Strip Set 2
Make 5.

4. Join the 1½"-wide segments randomly, so the prints don't match, to make nine-patch units.

Make 20.

5. Join four 6½"-wide segments and 3 embroidered squares to make each of 4 rows. Press the seam allowances toward the 6½"-wide segments.

Make 4 rows.

6. Join 4 nine-patch units and three 6½"-wide segments to make each of 5 rows. Press the seam allowances toward the 6½"-wide segments.

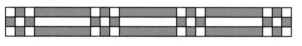

Make 5 rows.

7. Join the rows of blocks and the sashing rows, beginning and ending with rows containing nine-patch units.

8. Add the 4½" x 39½" border strips to the sides of the quilt top. Add the 4½" x 38½" border strips to the top and bottom of the quilt top.

9. Layer the quilt top with batting and backing. Quilt as desired.

10. Bind the edges with bias strips of fabric.

KITTY HOMEMAKER

KITTY HOMEMAKER by Nancy J. Martin, 1999, Woodinville, Washington, 59½" x 74½".
Quilted by Alvina Nelson, Salina, Kansas.

12" block

MATERIALS
42"-wide fabric

¾ yd. white solid for embroidery blocks

1 fat quarter each of 6 red prints for blocks*

1 fat quarter each of 6 red prints with white backgrounds
    for blocks*

1 fat quarter each of 6 green prints for blocks*

⅜ yd. light print for sashing squares

1⅛ yds. green print for sashing

1½ yds. red print for outer border

4 yds. for backing

⅝ yd. of fabric for 280" of bias binding

3 skeins of 6-strand embroidery floss in red

> ** The most economical way to purchase and cut fabric for this
> quilt is to make 2 identical blocks from each print. For a scrap-
> pier look, like the quilt shown on page 25, add more red or
> green prints.*

CUTTING

From the white solid, cut:

   12 squares, 7½" x 7½", for embroidery blocks

From each red fat quarter, cut:

   1 square (6 total), each 9" x 9", for bias squares

   1 square (6 total), each 8" x 8", for bias squares

   4 squares (24 total), each 4¼" x 4¼". Cut twice
       diagonally to yield 96 triangles.

From each red-with-white-background fat quarter, cut:

   1 square (6 total), each 9" x 9", for bias squares

   1 square (6 total), each 8" x 8", for bias squares

   4 squares (24 total), each 4¼" x 4¼". Cut twice
       diagonally to yield 96 triangles.

From each green fat quarter, cut:

   4 squares (24 total), each 4¼" x 4¼". Cut twice
       diagonally to yield 96 triangles.

From the light print, cut:

   2 strips, each 3½" x 42". Crosscut the strips into
       20 squares, each 3½" x 3½" for sashing
       squares.

From the green print, cut:

   3 strips, each 12½" x 42". Crosscut the strips into
       31 rectangles, each 3½" x 12½" for sashing
       strips.

From the red print, cut:

   7 strips, each 6" x 42", for outer border

DIRECTIONS

1. Transfer the Kitty Homemaker designs to the white
   squares. Embroider the designs and press the finished blocks. Trim the blocks to 6½" x 6½", centering the design.

2. Pair each 9" red square with a 9" red-with-white-
   background square, right sides up. Cut and sew 3¼"
   bias strips following directions for making bias
   squares on page 00. Cut 48 bias squares, each 3½"
   x 3½".

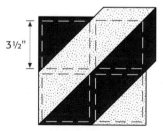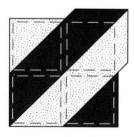

3½"

3. Pair each 8" red square with an 8" red-with-white-background square, right sides up. Cut and sew 2½" bias strips, following directions for making bias squares on page 00. Cut 48 bias squares, each 2½" x 2½".

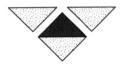

4. Join 2 red-with-white-background triangles and a 2½" bias square.

Make 4 matching units for each block.

5. Join 2 red and 2 green triangles and 1 unit from step 4.

Make 4 matching units for each block.

6. Join four 3½" bias squares, 4 units from step 5, and 1 embroidered square to make a block. Use matching red-with-white-background triangles, red triangles, and green triangles for each block.

Make 12.

7. Join 3 blocks and 4 sashing strips to make each of 4 rows. Press the seam allowances toward the sashing strips.

Make 4 rows.

8. Join 4 sashing squares and 3 sashing strips to make each of 5 rows. Press the seam allowances toward the sashing squares.

Make 5 rows.

9. Join the rows of blocks and sashing rows.

10. Join the 6"-wide red strips for the outer border and stitch them to the quilt top following directions on page 29.
11. Layer the quilt top with batting and backing. Quilt as desired.
12. Bind the edges with bias strips of fabric.

DISH TOWELS

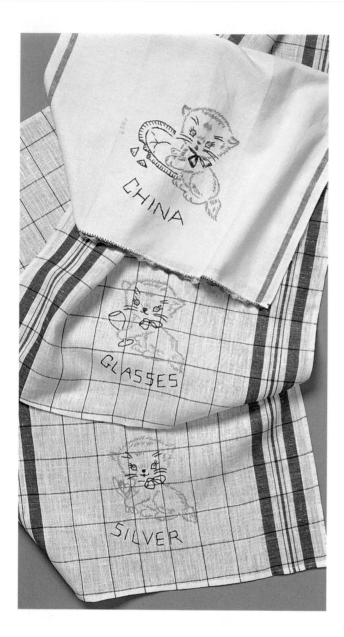

MATERIALS

3 ready-made dish towels
1 skein of 6-strand embroidery floss for each color used
    (blue, yellow, brown, pink, and gray)

DIRECTIONS

1. Transfer the Kitty Dish Towel designs onto the towels.
2. Embroider the designs.
3. Press the towels.

NOTE

If you purchased towel fabric by the yard, hem the unfinished ends before embroidering the designs. Fold the raw edges under ¼", then ¼" again and stitch.

Finishing Techniques

Borders

Straighten the edge of your quilt top before adding borders. There should be little or no trimming needed for a straight-set quilt.

To find the correct measurement for cut-to-fit border strips, always measure through the center of the quilt, not at the outside edges. This ensures that the borders are of equal length on opposite sides of the quilt and brings the outer edges into line with the center dimension if discrepancies exist. Otherwise, your quilt might not be "square" due to minor piecing variations and/or stretching that occurred while you worked with the pieces. If there is a large difference between the two sides, it is better to go back and correct the source of the problem than to try to make the border fit and end up with a distorted quilt.

Plain borders are commonly cut along the crosswise grain and seamed where extra length is needed. The seam will be less noticeable and stronger if it is pieced on an angle. You may need additional fabric to piece on the angle.

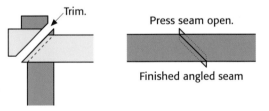

Trim.

Press seam open.

Finished angled seam

Borders cut from the lengthwise grain of fabric require extra yardage, but seaming to achieve the required length is then unnecessary.

Straight-Cut Corners

The easiest border to add is a straight-cut border. This method has been used on the quilts with borders in this book. You will save fabric if you attach the border to the longer sides first, then stitch the border to the remaining two sides.

1. Measure the length of the quilt at the center. Cut two border strips to this measurement, piecing as necessary. Mark the centers of the border strips and the quilt top.

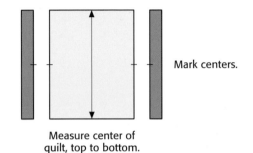

Mark centers.

Measure center of quilt, top to bottom.

2. Pin the borders to the sides of the quilt, matching centers and ends and easing or slightly stretching the quilt to fit the border strip as necessary.

3. Sew the side borders in place and press the seams toward the borders.

4. Measure the center width of the quilt, including the side borders, to determine the length of the top and bottom borders. Cut two border strips to this measurement, piecing strips as necessary. Mark the centers of the border strips and the quilt top.

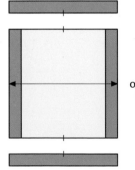

Measure center of quilt, side to side, including borders.

Mark centers.

5. Pin borders to the top and bottom of the quilt top, easing or slightly stretching the quilt to fit as necessary. Sew the top and bottom borders in place and press the seams toward the borders.

Marking the Quilt

You'll need to mark a design to be quilted on the quilt top unless you are doing one of the following: quilting in the ditch, outlining the design ¼" from all seams, or stitching a grid of straight lines using ¼"-wide masking tape as a guide.

To stitch in the ditch, place the stitches in the valley created next to the seam. Stitch on the side that does not have the seam allowance under it.

Quilting in the ditch

To outline a design, stitch ¼" from the seam inside each shape.

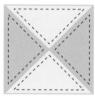

Outline quilting

To mark a grid or pattern of lines, use ¼" wide masking tape in 15" to 18" lengths. Place strips of tape on a small area and quilt next to the edge of the tape. Remove the tape when stitching is complete. You can reuse the tape to mark another area.

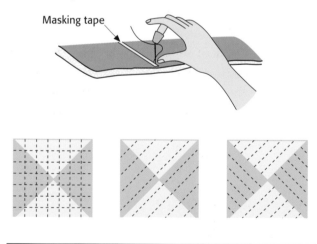

Masking tape

CAUTION

Don't leave tape on a quilt top for an extended length of time; it may leave a sticky residue.

To mark complex designs, use a stencil. Quilting stencils made from durable plastic are available in quilt shops. Use stencils to mark repeated designs. There is a groove cut in the plastic, wide enough to allow the use of a marking device. Just place the marker inside the groove to quickly transfer the design to the fabric. Good removable marking pencils include Berol Silver pencils, EZ Washout marking pencils, mechanical pencils, and sharp lead pencils. Just be sure to draw lines lightly. Test the removal of any marking device before marking your fabric.

Backing

For most quilts larger than crib size, you will need to piece the backing from two or more strips of fabric if you use 42"-wide fabric. Seams can run horizontally (crosswise join) or vertically (lengthwise join) in a pieced backing, as long as the fabric isn't a directional print. Avoid the temptation to use a bed sheet for a backing, as it is difficult to quilt through. Cut backing 3" to 4" larger than quilt top all around. Be sure to trim away the selvages where pieces are joined.

Sometimes the backing fabric is just a little too narrow for a quilt. Pieced backs are fun to make, and they can be the answer to this annoying problem. You can also use scraps of fabric from your sewing stash, piecing them together to form a backing large enough for your quilt top. This is most effective when you use some of the fabrics that were used on the front of the quilt.

If you plan to hang your quilt, you will need to put a sleeve or rod pocket on the back of the quilt (see page 35). Purchase extra backing fabric so that the sleeve and the backing match.

Batting

There are many types of batting to choose from. Select a high-loft batting for a bed quilt that you want to look puffy. Lightweight battings are fine for baby quilts or wall hangings. A lightweight batting is easier to quilt through and shows the quilting design well. It also resembles antique quilts, giving an old-fashioned look.

Polyester batting works well, doesn't shift after washing, and is easy to quilt through. It comes in lightweight, regular, and high lofts.

Cotton batting is a good choice if you are quilting an old quilt top. Most cotton batting must be quilted with stitches no more than 2" apart. There are, however, several new cotton battings available today which may be quilted up to 8" apart. Be sure to read the manufacturer's directions to determine the type of batting you have.

LAYERING AND BASTING

Open a package of batting and smooth it out flat. Allow the batting to rest in this position for at least twenty-four hours. Cut batting 3" to 4" larger than quilt top.

Press the backing so that all seams are flat and the fold lines have been removed. Place the backing on the table with the wrong side of the fabric facing up. If the table is large enough, you may want to tape the backing down with masking tape. Spread your batting over the backing, centering it, and smooth out any remaining folds.

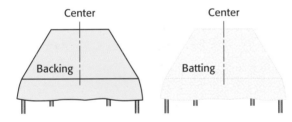

Center the freshly pressed and marked quilt top on these two layers. Check all four sides to make sure there is adequate batting and backing. Stretch the backing to make sure it is still smooth.

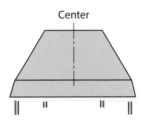

The basting method you use depends on whether you will quilt by hand or by machine. Thread basting is generally used for hand quilting, while safety-pin basting is used for machine quilting.

THREAD BASTING

Starting in the middle of the quilt top, baste the three layers together with straight pins while gently smoothing out the fullness to the sides and corners. Take care not to distort the straight lines of the quilt design and the borders.

After pinning, baste the layers together with a needle and light-colored thread. (Dark-colored thread may bleed onto the quilt.) Start in the middle and make a line of long stitches to each corner to form a large **X**.

Continue basting in a grid of parallel lines 6" to 8" apart. Finish with a row of basting around the outside edges. Quilts that are to be quilted with a hoop or on your lap will be handled more than those quilted on a frame; therefore, they require more basting. After basting, remove the pins. Now you are ready to quilt.

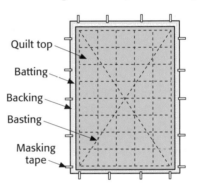

PIN BASTING

A quick way to baste a quilt top is with size 2 safety pins. They are large enough to catch all three layers but not so large that they snag fine fabric. Begin pinning in the center and work out toward the edges. Place pins 4" to 5" apart.

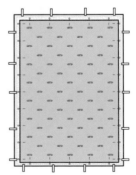

Baste around the outside edge to hold everything in place.

HAND QUILTING

To quilt by hand, you need quilting thread, quilting needles, small scissors, a thimble, and perhaps a balloon or large rubber band to help grasp the needle if it gets stuck. Quilt on a frame, a large hoop, or on your lap or a table. Use a single strand of quilting thread no longer than 18". Make a small, single knot at the end of the thread. The quilting stitch is a small running stitch that goes through all three layers of the quilt. Take two, three, even four stitches at a time if you can keep them even. When crossing seams, you might find it necessary to "hunt and peck" one stitch at a time.

To begin, insert the needle in the top layer about 1" from the point you want to start stitching. Pull the needle out at the starting point and gently tug at the knot until it pops through the fabric and is buried in the batting. Make a backstitch and begin quilting. Stitches should be tiny (eight to ten per inch is good), even, and straight; tiny will come with practice.

When you come almost to the end of the thread, make a single knot ¼" from the fabric. Take a backstitch to bury the knot in the batting. Run the thread off through the batting and out the quilt top; then snip it off. The first and last stitches will look different from the running stitches in between. To make them less noticeable, start and stop where quilting lines cross each other or at seam joints.

Hand-quilting stitch

MACHINE QUILTING

A walking foot or even-feed foot is essential for straight-line and grid quilting and for large, simple curves. It helps feed the quilt layers through the machine without shifting or puckering. Read the machine instruction manual for special tension settings to sew through extra fabric thicknesses.

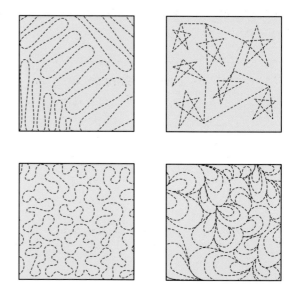

Walking foot attachment

For more intricately curved designs, you need to use a darning foot and lower the feed dogs. This is called free-motion quilting because the fabric moves freely under the foot of the sewing machine. Because the feed dogs are lowered, the stitch length is determined by the speed at which you run the machine and feed the fabric under the foot. Practice running the machine fairly fast, since this makes it easier to sew smoother lines of quilting. With free-motion quilting, do not turn the fabric under the needle. Instead, guide the fabric as if it were under a stationary pencil (the needle). With a little practice, you can imitate beautiful hand-quilting designs quickly.

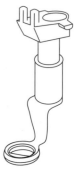

Darning foot

Practice first on a layer of fabric scraps until you get the feel of controlling the motion of the fabric with your hands. Stitch some free-form scribbles, zigzags, and curves. Try a heart or a star. Free-motion quilting may feel awkward at first, but with a little determination and practice, you will be able to complete a project in just a few hours.

Keep the spacing between quilting lines consistent over the entire project. Avoid using complex, little designs and leaving large spaces unquilted. With most battings, a 2" to 3" square is the largest area that can be left unquilted. When all the quilting has been completed, remove the safety pins. Sometimes it is necessary to remove safety pins as you work.

Do not try to machine quilt an entire quilt in one sitting, even if it's a small quilt. Break the work into short periods and stretch and relax your muscles regularly.

BINDING

My favorite quilt binding is a double-fold French binding made from bias strips. It rolls over the edges of the quilt nicely, and the two layers of fabric resist wear. If you use 2¼"-wide strips, the finished width of this binding will be ⅜".

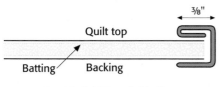

Double-fold French binding

To determine how much binding you'll need, measure the distance around your quilt and add about 10" for turning the corners and for overlapping the ends of the binding strips. The quilt directions tell you how much fabric to purchase for binding. If, however, you enlarge your quilt or need to compute binding fabric, use this handy chart:

LENGTH OF BINDING	FABRIC NEEDED
115"	¼ yd.*
180"	⅜ yd.*
255"	½ yd.
320"	⅝ yd.
400"	¾ yd.
465"	⅞ yd.

It is a good idea to purchase ½ yard of fabric instead of ¼ or ⅜ yard so the bias strips will be longer and the binding won't have as many seams.

After quilting, trim excess batting and backing even with the edge of the quilt top. A rotary cutter and long ruler will ensure accurate straight edges. If the basting is no longer in place, baste all three layers together at the outside edges. If you are going to attach a sleeve to the back of your quilt for hanging, turn to page 35 and attach it now, before you bind the edges.

To cut bias strips:

1. Align the 45° marking of the Bias Square along the selvage and place the ruler's edge against the square. Make the first cut.

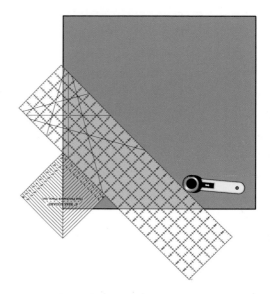

2. Measure the width of the strip, 2¼", from the cut edge of the fabric. Cut along the edge of the ruler.

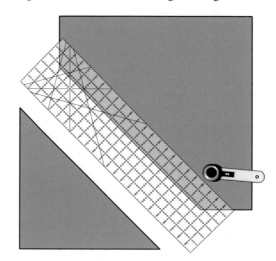

When cutting bias strips, a 24"-long ruler may be too short for some of the cuts. After making several cuts, carefully fold the fabric over itself so that the bias edges are even. Continue to cut bias strips.

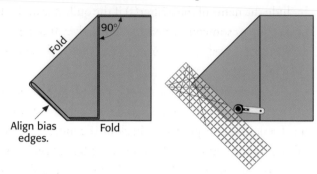

Follow these steps to bind the edges:

1. Stitch bias strips together, offsetting them as shown. Press the seams open.

2. Fold the strip in half lengthwise, wrong sides together, and press.

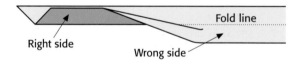

3. Unfold the binding at one end and turn under ¼" at a 45° angle as shown.

4. Beginning on one side of the quilt, stitch the binding to the quilt, using a ¼"-wide seam allowance. Start stitching 1" to 2" from the start of the binding. Stop stitching ¼" from the corner and backstitch.

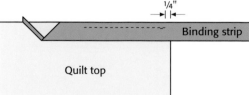

5. Turn the quilt to prepare the sewing along the next edge. Fold the binding away from the quilt, then fold again to place the binding along the second edge of the quilt. This fold creates an angled pleat at the corner.

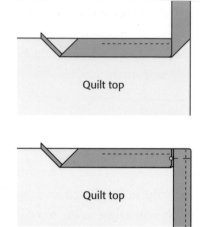

6. Stitch from the fold of the binding along the second edge of the quilt top, stopping ¼" from the corner as you did for the first corner; backstitch. Repeat the stitching and mitering process on the remaining edges and corners of the quilt.

7. When you reach the beginning of the binding, cut the end 1" longer than needed and tuck the end inside the beginning. Stitch the rest of the binding.

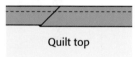

8. Turn the binding to the back side, over the raw edges of the quilt. Blindstitch in place, with the folded edge covering the row of machine stitching. At each corner, fold the binding to form a miter on the back of the quilt.

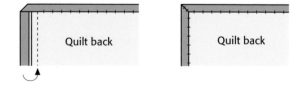

QUILT SLEEVES

If you plan to hang your quilt, attach a sleeve or rod pocket to the back before attaching the binding. From the leftover backing fabric, cut an 8"-wide strip of fabric equal to the width of your quilt. You may need to piece two or three strips together for larger quilts. On each end, fold over ½" and then fold ½" again. Press and stitch by machine.

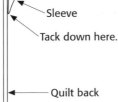

½"   ½"

Fold the strip in half lengthwise, wrong sides together; baste the raw edges to the top edge of the back of your quilt. These will be secured when you sew on the binding. Your quilt should be about 1" wider than the sleeve on both sides. Make a little pleat in the sleeve to accommodate the thickness of the rod, then slipstitch the ends and bottom edge of the sleeve to the backing fabric. This keeps the rod from being inserted next to the quilt backing.

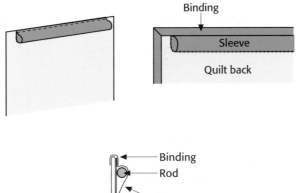

Binding

Sleeve

Quilt back

Binding

Rod

Sleeve

Tack down here.

Quilt back

QUILT LABELS

It's a good idea to label a quilt with its name, the name and address of the maker, and the date it was made. Include the name of the quilter(s) if the quilt was quilted by a group or someone other than the maker. If the quilt is being presented to someone as a gift, also include that information.

To make a label, use a permanent-ink pen to print or legibly write all this information on a piece of muslin. Press freezer paper to the back of the muslin to stabilize it while you write. Press the raw edges of the muslin to the wrong side of the label. Remove the freezer paper and stitch the label securely to the lower corner of the back of the quilt. You can also do labels in cross-stitch or embroidery.

ABOUT THE AUTHOR

Nancy J. Martin, talented author, teacher, and quiltmaker, has written more than thirty books on quiltmaking. Nancy is an innovator in the quilting industry and introduced the Bias Square cutting ruler to quilters everywhere. Along with more than twenty years of teaching experience and numerous classic quilting titles to her credit, Nancy is the founder and president of Martingale & Company, the publisher of America's Best-Loved Quilt Books®. When not piecing quilts, she enjoys redwork embroidery and is now compiling over two hundred redwork designs to be offered on a CD-ROM. Nancy and her husband, Dan, enjoy living in the Pacific Northwest.

RESOURCES

Sinema, Laurene. *Redwork: Quilts and More.* Fort Worth, Tex.: Design Originals, 1999.

Weiss, Rita. *Learn to do Redwork.* San Marcos, Calif.: American School of Needlework, 1999.

Woodard, Thos. K., and Blanche Greenstein. *Twentieth Century Quilts, 1900–1950.* New York: E. P. Dutton, l988.

PATTERNS

Use the patterns on pages 37–48 with a lead or transfer pencil. The patterns beginning on page 49 are hot-iron transfers.

GARDEN

CHINA

GLASSES

SILVER

HOT IRON TRANSFERS

To use the hot iron transfers, you'll need a dry iron set for cotton. Center the transfer on the fabric. With firm pressure, hold the iron in place for about ten seconds. Do not move the iron back and forth or you will blur the lines. If the design is large, move the iron and hold again for about ten seconds. Repeat until the whole design is transferred. Be sure to place the transfer exactly where you want it on the fabric and cover all lines with embroidery stitches. The transfer ink is permanent and will not wash out. Transfers can be used several times. Use the transfers on this page to experiment.